The Secret to Dim

A Cookbook of Thirty Easy Dim Sum Dishes

BY: Ivy Hope

Copyright © 2020 by Ivy Hope

Copyright/License Page

Please don't reproduce this book. It means you are not allowed to make any type of copy (print or electronic), sell, publish, disseminate or distribute. Only people who have written permission from the author are allowed to do so.

This book is written by the author taking all precautions that the content is true and helpful. However, the reader needs to be careful about his/her action. If anything happens due to the reader's actions the author won't be taken as responsible.

Table of Contents

Introduction 6

   An Easy Start 8

   Early Dessert - Cantonese Steamed Custard Buns 11

   Chinese Spring Rolls 14

   Chinese BBQ Pork Buns - To Warm Your Soul 17

   Beef Curry Puffs 20

   A Long Journey to Taste bud Heaven 23

   Sticky Rice Lotus Leaf Wraps 26

   Tripe Stew 29

   A Classic - Vegetable Dumplings 32

   Watercress Steamed Meatballs - The Healthiest of Them All 35

   Vegan Chinese Tofu Buns 38

   Taro Cake 41

   Simplicity - Sticky Rice with Chinese Sausage 43

   The Roll of All Rolls 46

The Palate Pleaser. 50

You're Shumai Type 52

Sticky Rice Mushroom Shumai 55

Soup Dumplings 58

I've got Fillings for You 61

All Wrapped Up 64

Let's Make It Shiny 66

Chinese Pork Potstickers 69

A Yellow Surprise 72

Chinese Stuffed Tofu 75

Turnip Cake - An Interesting Twist 77

Clear as Crystal Dumplings 80

Steamed Pork Buns 83

Zhaliang - Bread Rolls Reinvented 86

Bamboozled 89

Go Green 92

Conclusion 95

About the Author 96

Author's Afterthoughts 97

Introduction

People say cooking is an art, and art has a technique. Emboldening both these statements is the fine, slightly complicated art of Asian cooking. Nevertheless, like a well-practiced dancer, you will be able to go through the motions of creating these complicated food items fluently once you try multiple times. Why should you try?

Well, because the flavors and texture of the results are so delectable, your eyes will flutter shut in contentment.

Don't believe us? We're here to prove you wrong with a master cookbook of Dim Sum varieties, enough to feed a hungry army and to win hearts with your expertise. From rolls to dumplings, easy short recipes to ones that take more than a day, we have it all lined up just for you. Once you delve into this cookbook, you will re-emerge more knowledgeable, wiser, and definitely a better cook.

Don't wait any longer, get your steamers ready, head straight to your nearest Asian market, and grab your ingredients! It's time to cook some Dim Sums!

An Easy Start

We'll begin by using a shortcut method to cook one of the dishes that take an extremely long time to be prepped, and that is a Congee. It is a porridge served with pork and a thousand-year-old egg, beaten piping hot, and full of healthy ingredients. But we're going to break down the long preparation time to 20 minutes. For that, you'll have to prep the rice beforehand. Take a look!

Ingredients:

- White rice - ¾ cup
- Pork shoulder - 4 ounces, julienned
- Cornstarch - ½ teaspoon
- Oyster sauce - 1 teaspoon
- Vegetable oil - 1 teaspoon
- Water or chicken broth - 7 cups
- Thousand-year-old eggs - 2
- Ginger - 3 slices
- White pepper - ¼ teaspoon, ground
- Salt - as per taste
- Scallions - ¼ cup for garnishing
- Cilantro - ¼ Cup for garnishing

Preparation Time: 30 mins

Serving Size: 6

Instructions:

1. Refrigerate washed and drained white rice in a ziplock bag or freezer-safe box for over eight hours.

2. Make a marinade with cornstarch, vegetable oil and oyster sauce and marinade pork for twenty minutes.

3. Bring 7 cups of water or chicken broth to a boil and add the frozen rice into it. Let it come to a boil again, and simmer for fifteen minutes. Keep stirring to avoid the sticking of the rice to the bottom of the pot.

4. Meanwhile, dice the thousand-year-old egg and julienne the ginger into very thin slices.

5. Once fifteen minutes are up, add the pork, egg, and ginger and simmer for five minutes more. Mix in the pepper and salt and serve with garnishes. Enjoy!

Early Dessert - Cantonese Steamed Custard Buns

Yes, it might be too early to dive into a dessert recipe when there's so much savory left to explore, but this one is so mouthwatering that we just had to bring it to you immediately! For a steamed custard bun, dim sum style; check out the recipe below... and make sure you share it with others!

Ingredients:

Filling:

- Eggs - 2
- Powdered sugar - ½ cup
- Milk - ¼ cup
- Heavy cream - 3 tablespoons
- All-purpose flour - 3 tablespoons
- Cornstarch - ¼ cup
- Milk powder - ¼ cup
- Melted butter - 2 tablespoons

Dough:

- Yeast - 1 teaspoon
- Water - ¼ cup, warm
- All-purpose flour - 1½ cups
- Powdered sugar - 3 tablespoons
- Salt - ¼ teaspoon
- Coconut milk - 3 tablespoons
- Milk - 3 tablespoons

Preparation Time: 3 hours, 15 minutes

Serving Size: 12

Instructions:

1. Set up some water in a pan and let it boil, then simmer. In a bowl, pile in the eggs and sugar and beat for a minute, then combine the milk and heavy cream in it. Mix in the flour, milk powder and cornstarch and then add the melted butter.

2. Place this bowl in the pan and stir quickly and continuously until it thickens into a custard. Take off the heat and cool.

3. In another big bowl add yeast in 1/4th cup water and let it sit for fifteen minutes until you see bubbles on the top.

4. Mix with this the flour, sugar, coconut milk and salt. Slowly combine regular milk into this until a smooth non-sticky dough is formed. Let it proof under a dry towel in a warm place for an hour until it doubles or triples in size.

5. Divide custard into 12 portions and shape them into balls.

6. Knead the proofed dough for two more minutes to get rid of air bubbles, then transfer to a clean floured surface. Divide into twelve portions and roll out each portion into circles, edges thinner than the center.

7. Place the custard filling in the center and pleat the edges close. Place them on parchment paper in a steamer and let them proof for fifteen more minutes.

8. Once proofed, turn on the heat and steam for 12 minutes. Once done, let them sit covered in the steamer, off the heat for five more minutes to cool and hold shape. Serve hot.

Chinese Spring Rolls

Alright back to some savory snacks. Spring rolls are a favorite in every house among the kids, but were you making them, right? Well, here's a way to find out and make some authentic Chinese spring rolls, just for your family. Take a look at this beautiful recipe for some crunchy rolls!

Ingredients:

Pork:

- Pork loin - 8 ounces, finely shredded
- Salt - ¼ teaspoon
- Sesame oil - ½ teaspoon
- Shaoxing wine - 1 teaspoon
- Cornstarch - ½ teaspoon
- White pepper - ¼ teaspoon

Filling:

- Oil - 2 tablespoons
- Garlic - 1 clove, minced
- shiitake mushrooms - 10, dried, then soaked and thinly sliced
- Carrots - 1 cup, julienned
- Bamboo shoots - 1 cup, julienned
- Napa cabbage - 6 cups, julienned
- Shaoxing wine - 1 tablespoon
- Soy sauce - 2 tablespoons
- Sesame oil - 1 teaspoon
- Salt and pepper - as per taste
- Sugar - 1/4th tablespoon
- 2 tablespoons cornstarch in 2 tablespoons cold water, dissolved.

Wrapping:

- Spring roll wrappers - 1 package
- Frying Oil - 2-3 cups

Dipping sauce:

- Sugar - 2 teaspoons
- Hot water - 2 teaspoons
- Worcestershire sauce - 1 teaspoon
- Soy sauce - 1 tablespoon

Preparation Time: 1 hour 20 minutes

Serving Size: 18

Instructions:

1. Marinade the pork with the rest of the ingredients given and let it sit for thirty minutes.

2. Let the pork cook in two tablespoons of oil until it turns brown and then add garlic, carrots, and mushrooms and stir for thirty seconds or so. Next, add the napa cabbage, wine, and bamboo shoots and stir for a minute. Let it simmer.

3. Add the sesame oil, white pepper, salt, sugar and soy sauce.

4. Stir for three minutes or so and then add the cornstarch slurry and cook till there is no water left.

5. Cool the filling in the fridge, it will be easier to handle while rolling. Meanwhile, make the dipping sauce by heating all the ingredients in a pan and letting them mix and simmer.

6. Layout the spring roll wrapper, add a spoonful of filling and roll it into a cigar shape. Use cornstarch slurry to seal it together.

7. Fry them in oil until they turn a golden-brown color and then transfer them to paper towels.

8. Serve hot with the dipping sauce and Enjoy!

Chinese BBQ Pork Buns - To Warm Your Soul

A hot steaming bun fresh out of the oven... you can even feel the warmth in your mouth as you try to eat it. This pork bun recipe is one of the most delicious buns of all time, and you'll know from the aroma when you're in the process of making them. Make sure you don't burn your tongue from your eagerness to take a bite. Dive right in!

Ingredients:

Bun:

- Bread flour -5 &1/3 cups
- Water - 2/3 cup
- Milk - 1 & 1/3 cup
- Sugar - 1/3 cup
- Salt - 1 teaspoon
- Instant yeast - 4 teaspoons
- Eggs - 2
- Butter - 4 tablespoons, melted
- Egg wash - 1 egg, beaten with a tablespoon of milk
- Sesame seeds - 1 tablespoon

Filling:

- Oil - 2 tablespoons
- Shallots - 1/2 cup, finely chopped
- Sugar - 2 tablespoons
- Soy sauce - 1 ½ tablespoon
- Oyster sauce - 2 tablespoons
- Sesame oil - 2 teaspoons
- Dark soy sauce - 2 teaspoons
- Chicken stock - ¾ cup
- Flour - 3 tablespoons
- Chinese barbecue pork - 1 cup

Preparation Time: 3 hours

Serving Size: 16

Instructions:

1. Mix ⅓ cup milk, ⅓ cup flour, and ⅔ cup water and mix over medium heat until it forms a thick paste.

2. Mix 5 cups of flour, salt, sugar and yeast, and add the flour paste. Mix in 1 cup milk, melted butter, and 2 eggs and knead for 15-20 minutes. Let the dough rest as a ball in a greased bowl covered by damp cloth and rise for an hour.

3. Stir fry onions in a pan for two minutes, then add the sugar, sesame oil, oyster sauce, soy sauce, and dark soy and stir for a couple of minutes. Then add the chicken stock and flour and stir till it thickens slightly. Remove from heat, mix in the pork and let it cool.

4. Preheat the oven to 400F. Separate dough into 16 pieces and spread into little balls, thinner at ends and thick at the center. Lay in the filling and crimp them shut and lay them in baking sheets, seal side down.

5. Do the egg wash and sprinkle sesame seeds. Turn the oven to 350F and bake for 25 mins, until golden brown.

Beef Curry Puffs

You hear beef curry puffs, and you think it's spicy. After this recipe, though, you're going to fondly remember it as a mouth-watering and delicious puff, with a hot, delectable beef curry waiting inside. Baking has never been easier. Try out this beef curry puff recipe and surprise the people in your life with your cooking skills and varied cuisines!

Ingredients:

- Vegetable oil - 3 tablespoons
- Onion - 1, finely diced
- Garlic - 2 cloves, minced
- Ground beef - 1 pound
- Curry powder - 2 tablespoons
- Turmeric powder - 1½ teaspoons
- Cumin powder - ½ teaspoon
- Sugar - ¼ teaspoon
- Black pepper - ¼ teaspoon
- Salt - 1 teaspoon
- Beef broth - 2/3 cup
- Cornstarch - 1 tablespoon
- Puff pastry - 17 ounces, 2 sheets
- 1 egg beaten mixed with 1 tablespoon water

Preparation Time: 2 hours 30 minutes

Serving Size: 18

Instructions:

1. Cook onions and garlic in a pan in oil until translucent.

2. Add ground beef, let it turn brown, and then mix the curry powder, salt, turmeric, black pepper, sugar and cumin and cook for a minute or two.

3. Mix beef broth with one tablespoon cornstarch and make a slurry and mix it with the beef. Let it thicken until there is no water. Let it cool.

4. Cut puff pastry into 9 squares and spoon three tablespoons of the filling into it, and seal as a triangle by crimping the edges. Refrigerate for fifteen minutes and preheat oven to 400 F

5. Brush puffs with egg wash and bake them for eighteen minutes. Let it cool before serving.

A Long Journey to Taste bud Heaven

All good things take time, and sometimes that's true for cooking as well. Dim Sum recipes are known for their complexity and flavors, along with their preparation time that can last pretty long. However, it's nothing to fear, because the results will leave you blown away. Here's a delicious beef short ribs recipe that seems daunting but is actually quite simple!

Ingredients:

- Beef short ribs - 1 pound
- Salt - ½ teaspoon
- Baking soda - ¼ teaspoon
- Sugar - ¼ teaspoon
- Shaoxing wine - 1 tablespoon
- Light soy sauce - 1 teaspoon
- Dark soy sauce - ¼ teaspoon
- Oyster sauce - 1 teaspoon
- Sesame oil - ½ teaspoon
- Garlic - ½ clove
- Red onion - 1, thinly sliced
- Oil - 1 teaspoon
- Cornstarch - 2 teaspoons
- Black pepper - ½ teaspoon, ground

Preparation Time: 12hours 10 minutes

Serving Size: 4

Instructions:

1. Clean the ribs properly and mix all the ingredients listed from salt to garlic. This forms the marinade. Marinate the beef and red onion with it and keep it in the refrigerator overnight.

2. The next day, take the beef out of the refrigerator, let it come to room temperature and add the oil, cornstarch and black pepper.

3. Set up your steamer to a gentle boil. Wait for it to preheat and then steam the ribs for ten minutes. Serve hot and enjoy!

Sticky Rice Lotus Leaf Wraps

Sticky rice is so easy to cook, you'll be surprised at how little attention it needs. But lotus wraps? If that's something you've never heard of before, rest assured, you're going to love it. Wrapping the rice in these leaves gives it an exquisite flavor that will take the dish to levels beyond comprehension. And the best part is, it's really easy to make! Take a look.

Ingredients:

Marinade:

- Light soy sauce - 2 tablespoons
- White pepper - 1/2 teaspoon, ground
- Oyster sauce - 1 tablespoon
- Five-spice powder - 1/2 teaspoon
- Ginger - 1 tablespoon, finely chopped
- Shaoxing wine - 1 tablespoon
- Cornstarch - 1 teaspoon

Others:

- Boneless chicken thighs - 4, in chunks
- Sticky rice - 4 cups
- Dark soy sauce - 2 tablespoons
- Oil - 4 tablespoons plus extra 1 teaspoon for wrapping
- Mushrooms - 6 cups
- Scallion - 3 cups, chopped
- Sea salt - 1 teaspoon
- 5 whole lotus leaves

Preparation Time: 4 hours 30 minutes

Serving Size: 10

Instructions:

1. Soak the lotus leaves in warm water for an hour, cut off stems and rinse them well and cut in halves.

2. Mix the marinade ingredients together and coat the chicken chunks in it well and let it marinate in the refrigerator until the time comes to use them.

3. Soak the rice in water for two hours, drain it and mix with two tablespoons of soy sauce.

4. Stir fry mushrooms in your skillet or wok and let them cook for a while. Once they are done, do the same for the chicken, cook it until it browns and then mix in the mushrooms, scallion, and salt. Let the flavors combine on heat.

5. Mix the chicken with the soaked rice and prepare the lotus leaves for wrapping. Brush some oil onto one section of the leaf at an end, and spoon about 3/4th of a cup of the rice mixture onto that section. Wrap into a rectangular shape and tie it up with string.

6. Steam for ninety minutes. Serve hot with some chili oil and enjoy it!

Tripe Stew

Tripe is well known to make the stomach turn, excuse the pun, but it is a widely used ingredient in Chinese cooking and has the same chewy texture as calamari. Use it in a way that makes its flavors pop and smell amazing; you will have a great dish in your hands that is sure to be a household favorite. Who doesn't like stew anyway? Give this recipe a try and introduce a new ingredient to your kitchen!

Ingredients:

Tripe:

- Honeycomb beef tripe - 2 lbs. fresh
- Water - 8 cups
- Salt - 2 teaspoons
- Ginger - 2 slices, smashed
- Scallion - 1, cut and smashed.
- Shaoxing wine - 2 tablespoons

Others:

- Oil - 1 tablespoon
- Ginger - 3 slices smashed
- Star anise - 4
- Daikon radish - 1
- Shaoxing wine - 1 tablespoon
- Light soy sauce - 1/4 cup
- Dark soy sauce - 1/4 teaspoon
- Light brown sugar - 1 tablespoon
- Water - 2 &1/2 cups
- Sesame oil - 1 teaspoon
- White pepper - 1/8 teaspoon
- Salt - as per taste
- Cornstarch - 1 tablespoon mixed with 1 tablespoon water
- Scallion - 1, chopped

Preparation Time: 1 hour 45 minutes

Serving Size: 8

Instructions:

1. Rinse the tripe under cold water. Transfer it to a wok, add water, salt, ginger, wine and scallion and let it come to a boil. Then turn off the heat and let it rest for five minutes. Next, rinse the tripe in water and let it drain.

2. Once cooled, cut it into pieces. Meanwhile, in a wok, add oil, star anise, and ginger and cook for thirty seconds, then turn to high heat and add the tripe immediately and cook for two minutes. Once done mix it with Shaoxing wine for 30 seconds.

3. Now mix soy sauce, water, brown sugar, and white pepper into this and bring to a boil. Then let it simmer for 20 minutes, stirring continuously.

4. Add turnips and cook for twenty minutes more, or longer if you want them more tender. Lastly, bring the dish to a boil and add the cornstarch slurry along with the scallions and let it thicken. Serve hot and enjoy!

A Classic - Vegetable Dumplings.

We've made congee, a roll, a dessert, even a rice dish wrapped in a leaf! But we think it's about time we get to the real reason why anyone would want to try dim sum, for the folks who associate it with their favorite dish, the Momo's close cousin: Dumplings. Here's a classic vegetable dumpling recipe that will leave you gorging on more. Remember, it's all in the pleating!

Ingredients:

- Dumpling wrappers:
- All-purpose flour - 3 &1/2 cups
- Water - 1 cup (plus 2 tablespoons), tepid

Filling:

- Oil - 3 tablespoons (plus ¼ cup)
- Ginger - 1 tablespoon, minced
- Onion - 1, chopped
- Shiitake mushrooms - 2 cups, chopped
- Cabbage - 1 &1/2 cups, finely shredded
- Carrot - 1 &1/2 cups, finely shredded
- Garlic chives - 1 cup, finely chopped
- White pepper - 1/2 teaspoon
- Sesame oil - 2 teaspoons
- Shaoxing wine - 3 tablespoons
- Soy sauce - 2 tablespoons
- Sugar - 1 teaspoon
- Salt - to taste

Preparation Time: 3 hours 20 minutes

Serving Size: 8

Instructions:

1. Knead the dough with water for 10 minutes till it is smooth. Cover with damp cloth and let it rest.

2. In a wok or pan add some oil and cook the ginger for half a minute until the aroma comes out. Then add the onions and cook them until translucent.

3. Add mushrooms and cook them for three to five minutes until they are tender and all their water has been cooked off. Next, add the carrots and cabbage and cook for two to three minutes till no liquid remains.

4. Transfer vegetable mixture to a bowl, add chives, soy sauce salt if needed, sugar, white pepper, sesame oil, and wine and mix well with ¼ cup of oil.

5. Cut dough into small chunks and roll them out into circles, the center thicker than the edges. Spoon a little filling inside and pleat them shut.

6. You can pan-fry them in some oil for two minutes. Drizzle some water into the pan and cover the lid and cook until it evaporates and then cook for another two minutes. Or, you can steam them for 15-20 minutes in your steamer. Serve hot and enjoy!

Watercress Steamed Meatballs - The Healthiest of Them All.

Meatballs bring a smile to your face, don't they? When we think of spaghetti and meatballs, and some of us may frown because they're a tiny bit unhealthy. But we are here to redirect your brainwaves into reimagining meatballs as a much healthier alternative: the watercress steamed meatballs. Full of flavor and everyone's best friend, you should definitely give this a try.

Ingredients:

- Beef chuck - 1 pound, fan untrimmed, ground or hand-chopped
- Water - 1/2 cup, cold
- Baking soda - 1/2 teaspoon
- Ginger - 1/2 teaspoon, finely minced
- Scallion whites - 1 teaspoon, finely minced
- Sugar - 1 teaspoon
- Salt - 1 &1/8 teaspoon
- Cornstarch - 1 tablespoon
- Vegetable oil - 1 tablespoon (plus 1 teaspoon)
- Sesame oil - 1/4 teaspoon
- Shaoxing wine - 2 teaspoons
- White pepper - 1/4 teaspoon
- Ground tangerine peel - 1 & 1/4 teaspoons
- Coriander powder - 1/4 teaspoon
- 1 egg white
- 2 bunches of fresh watercress
- Cilantro - 1/4 cup, finely chopped

Preparation Time: 1 hour 15 minutes

Serving Size: 6

Instructions:

1. Add the beef, water and baking powder in a bowl. Use an electric mixer or vigorously stir it yourself for around fifteen minutes. Take out the tough meat fiber sticking to the paddle or fork and make sure the fat and meat are well combined.

2. To this, mix the ginger, white pepper, sugar, salt, 1 tablespoon vegetable oil, sesame oil, wine, dried tangerine peel powder, coriander powder, egg white, scallions, and cornstarch. Stir for twenty minutes or more. Refrigerate this mixture overnight for the best flavor.

3. Blanch the watercress in water for 30 seconds and wash them in ice-cold water. Chop them very finely and incorporate them into the meat mixture. Make even balls out of the mixture.

4. Lay the remaining watercress in your steamer and pile the meatballs on top of it. Steam for 12 minutes on high. Enjoy!

Vegan Chinese Tofu Buns

We've made some delectable pork buns...wouldn't it be unfair if we left our vegan friends deprived of this delicious bun? Don't worry, we have you covered. Here's a vegan version of the Chinese buns, stuffed with delicious tofu. Try it out!

Ingredients:

Dough:

- Warm water- ½ cup + ½ cup
- Dry yeast - 1 teaspoon active
- Bread flour- 3 cups
- Coconut oil - ¼ cup
- Sugar - ½ cup
- Salt - a pinch

Filling:

- Oil - 2 tablespoons
- Onion - 1, diced
- Extra-firm tofu - 1 pound
- Soy sauce - 2 ½ tablespoons
- Dark soy sauce- ½ teaspoon
- Sugar - 1 tablespoon
- Salt - 1/2 teaspoon
- Sesame oil - 1 teaspoon
- Hoisin sauce - 1 tablespoon
- White pepper - 1 teaspoon
- Water or Vegetable stock - 1 ¼ cups
- Flour - 2 tablespoons

The coating on buns:

- Sugar - 1 tablespoon
- Warm water - 2 tablespoons

Preparation Time: 3 hours

Serving Size: 10 buns

Instructions:

1. Mix the yeast, ⅓ cup flour and ½ cup water in a bowl and set it aside to foam.

2. Add the coconut oil to the mixture and mix well. Then combine with the remaining water, remaining flour, salt, and sugar. Knead for 10 minutes and let it proof for an hour.

3. Meanwhile heat up a pan and oil fry the onions and tofu until it browns. Then add the soy sauces, salt, sugar, white pepper, and hoisin sauce and cook for two minutes. Then mix in the vegetable stock and corn flour and let it thicken. Set aside and cool before use.

4. Knead the dough for 2-3 minutes to get rid of any air bubbles and then divide them into ten balls. Keep them under a damp towel and roll out each, thicker at the center than the edges. Spoon 2 tablespoons of cool filling into the center and pleat it shut.

5. Set them under a damp towel to rest until you preheat the oven to 375F. Brush the buns with sugar water and then turn the oven to 350 before baking them. Bake for 25-30 minutes. Enjoy!

Taro Cake

A root vegetable in a cake? What's cooking without a little challenge anyway. Taro cake is one of the popular dim sum dishes that we will be tackling in this book. Stay tuned for the Turnip cake recipe, another interesting twist on the cake, further along in this book. For now, let's take a look at how to make a taro cake.

Ingredients:

- Oil - 3 tablespoons
- Chinese sausage - 3 links, chopped
- Dried shrimp - 1/2 cup, chopped
- Scallions - 2 cups, chopped
- Taro - 2 pounds, cubed
- Salt - 2 teaspoons
- White pepper powder - 1 teaspoon
- Sesame oil - 2 teaspoon
- Water - 2 & 1/2 cups (plus 1 1/2 cups)
- Rice flour - 2 & 1/2 cups
- Glutinous rice flour - 1 cup

Preparation Time: 1 hour thirty minutes

Serving Size: 12

Instructions:

1. In a wok, pan fry the Chinese sausage with some oil for two minutes, then add the shrimp and fry for a minute. Next, add scallions and taro and let that cook for three minutes. Season with salt, white pepper, and sesame oil. Next, add 2 ½ cups water and cover, let it cook for 8 minutes. Then set aside to cool.

2. In a bowl, mix the two rice flours, 1 ½ water, and the taro mix until well combined.

3. Oil two cake pans and divide mixture evenly between them. Cook them in a double-decker steamer for 45 minutes. Do a toothpick test, if it comes out clean, it's ready.

4. You can eat it as it is or pan sear it in oil for a few minutes before serving with oyster sauce or sprinkled with salt.

Simplicity - Sticky Rice with Chinese Sausage

Sometimes, all you need is a simple one-pot dish that's a warm rice meal, filled with flavor, and extremely easy to make. Fortunately, we have a dim sum dish that can double as a meal any time you wish. Let's dive into a recipe that blends Chinese sausage and sticky rice into one kitchen-friendly bowl.

Ingredients:

- Uncooked sticky rice - 2 cups
- Oyster sauce - 1 tablespoon
- Soy sauce - 1 ½ tablespoon
- Dark soy sauce - 2 teaspoons
- Sesame oil - ¼ teaspoon
- Chicken stock - ¼ cup
- Salt - ½ teaspoon
- Oil - 2 tablespoons
- Dried shrimp - ¼ cup (soaked for 15 minutes in warm water)
- Onion - 1, finely diced
- Dried shiitake mushrooms - 5 (soaked in warm water and diced)
- Chinese sausage - 3 links (cut into small discs)
- Shaoxing wine - 1 teaspoon
- White pepper - 1 teaspoon
- Scallions - 2, chopped
- Cilantro - ¼ cup, for garnishing

Preparation Time: 1 hour 15 minutes

Serving Size: 6

Instructions:

1. Cook sticky rice as per instructions on the rice packet and leave it to cool.

2. Combine oyster sauce, sesame oil, soy sauces, chicken stock, and salt. Heat your pan and stir fry the shrimp for a few seconds and then add the Chinese sausage, mushroom, and onions. Cook that for a minute, then add the wine and stir fry for two minutes.

3. Next, throw in the rice and add some of the sauce mixtures and fry it till it mixes well. Add the rest of the sauce, let it cook for a while and then serve hot and enjoy!

The Roll of All Rolls

Spring rolls are pretty popular in kitchens across the world, but have you heard of a rice noodle roll? This beautiful dish consists of shrimp wrapped in a supple rice noodle covering which is hand made. Now, the technique is a little tricky, but if you follow the instructions carefully, this is one dish that's easy to master. Give it a try!

Ingredients:

Shrimp:

- Shrimp - 8 ounces
- Water - 2 tablespoons
- Sugar - 1/2 teaspoon
- Baking soda - 1/8 teaspoon
- Sesame oil - 1/4 teaspoon
- Salt - 1/8 teaspoon
- Cornstarch - 1/2 teaspoon
- White pepper - 1/4 teaspoon

Sauce:

- Scallion - 1, white part
- Ginger - 6 slices
- Light soy sauce - 2 ½ tablespoons
- Dark soy sauce - 2 teaspoons
- Sugar - 5 teaspoons
- Water - 1/3 cup
- Oyster sauce - 1 teaspoon
- Oil - 1 teaspoon
- Salt- as per taste

Rice noodle rolls:

- Rice flour - 5 tablespoons
- Mung bean starch - 1 tablespoon
- Wheat starch - 2 tablespoons
- Cornstarch - 2 tablespoons
- Salt - 1/4 teaspoon
- Water - 1 cup
- Vegetable oil - 2 tablespoons

Preparation Time: 3 hours

Serving Size: 8

Instructions:

1. Coat the shrimp with water, baking powder and sugar and let it rest in the fridge for two hours.

2. Once done, take it out and wash under a stream of running water for five minutes.

3. Next, marinate it in sesame oil, white pepper, salt and cornstarch and leave it in the fridge till further use.

4. Make the sauce by combining all its ingredients in a wok and letting it simmer for a few minutes. When it is done, take out the lumps of scallion and ginger and store it.

5. Mix the rice flour, wheat starch, salt and mung bean starch in a bowl. Add water and mix till no lumps remain and let it rest to get rid of any air bubbles.

6. Soak a cotton cloth in water and also prepare your countertop by oiling it well for assembly of the roll.

7. Prepare your steamer and cook the shrimp on high for two minutes. Set them aside.

8. To steam rice noodles, use a sheet pan.

9. Line the cotton cloth on the pan and pour the noodle batter into it such that the cloth is just enveloped. Lower it into the steamer and take care to keep it leveled for uniform thickness of the rice noodle. Steam on high for two minutes and take it out.

10. Turn the pan upside down on your oiled surface such that the noodles touch the counter. Separate the noodles from the cloth using a scraper while both are still hot, do not worry about any aberrations.

11. Cut the noodles and line their edge with shrimp. Roll it up, cut and serve with the sauce. Enjoy!

The Palate Pleaser.

We have made a lot of savory dishes, and we think the time has come for some light, fluffy dessert options. The Chinese Steamed cake is a vanilla cake that's super moist and tender and melts in your mouth. What's even more interesting is that; it is made in a steamer, like most of the dim sum dishes. So, let's head straight to this easy recipe.

Ingredients:

- Eggs - 3, room temperature.
- Vegetable oil - ¼ cup
- Dark brown sugar - ¾ cup
- Vanilla extract - 1½ teaspoons
- Evaporated milk - ⅓ cup
- Vanilla pudding mix/custard powder - 1½ tablespoons
- Cake Flour - 1 cup
- Salt - ⅛ teaspoon
- Baking powder - 3½ teaspoons

Preparation Time: 1 hour 35 mins

Serving Size: 8

Instructions:

1. Beat the eggs, brown sugar and vegetable oil until fluffy.

2. Next, add vanilla extract, milk, custard powder and beat for a minute.

3. Sift the flour, salt and baking powder and fold it in. Let it rest for half an hour.

4. Grease your cake tin with butter and flour it. Or use parchment paper if you are using a steamer basket.

5. Pour the batter into the pan. Let it settle and even out for a few minutes. Meanwhile, set up your steamer. Steam for half an hour or an extra five minutes more on medium-high heat. Do a toothpick test to see if it is done if it comes out clean the cake is ready. Serve when cooled. Enjoy!

You're Shumai Type

Excuse the pun, but we just had to make it. Shumai or Siu Mai is a Chinese dish that resembles a dumpling but isn't quite so. This dish is dainty and pretty, but just as packed with flavor. Shumai is a classic addition to the dim sum spread, and it is a dish that takes only 40 minutes, which is quite a short time considering the other recipes we've seen earlier. Give this easy one and go to cook!

Ingredients:

Pork:

- Ground pork - 10 oz
- Sugar - 1 & 1/4 teaspoons
- White pepper - 1/4 teaspoon
- Cornstarch - 1 teaspoon
- Shaoxing wine - 1 tablespoon
- Light soy sauce - 1 tablespoon
- Water - 3 tablespoons
- Sesame oil - 1 teaspoon

Shrimp:

- Shrimp - 8 ounces
- Salt - 1/4 teaspoon
- Oil - 1/2 teaspoon

Finishing touches:

- Shiitake mushrooms - 3, soaked and finely chopped
- Ginger - 2 slices, grated
- Oyster sauce - 2 teaspoons
- Egg dumpling wrappers - 20, circular
- Frozen peas - 1 cup

Preparation Time: 40 mins

Serving Size: 5

Instructions:

1. Mix the pork with its marinade ingredients until it forms a nice paste. Mix the shrimp with salt and oil in another bowl and set that aside. Put both in the refrigerator until further use.

2. To make the filling, mix the mushrooms ginger and scallion along with the pork and shrimp mixtures in a large bowl. Add in oyster sauce and stir for five minutes until well combined.

3. Lightly oil the bottom of the steamer. Fill the dumpling wrappers with one tablespoon shumai filling and fold it up into its signature shape. Top with frozen peas and steam for 12 minutes on medium-high heat. Enjoy!

Sticky Rice Mushroom Shumai

This cookbook is all-inclusive; non-vegetarian, vegan, vegetarian, you name it, we have it. To help all our vegan and vegetarian friends get a taste of the wonderful Shumai, we have come up with a Vegan version. Take a look at this other Shumai recipe!

Ingredients:

Wrappers:

- All-purpose flour - 2 & 1/2 cups (plus extra for dusting)
- Salt - 1/2 teaspoon
- Boiling water - 3/4 cup

Filling:

- Uncooked sticky rice - 2 cups
- Oil - 1 tablespoon
- Dried shiitake mushrooms - 15 (soaked in warm water until softened, and diced)
- Shallots - 2, minced
- Scallions - 2, chopped
- Shaoxing wine - 1 tablespoon
- Salt - 1 teaspoon
- Soy sauce - 2 teaspoons
- Dark soy sauce - 1 teaspoon
- Five-spice powder - 1/8 teaspoon
- Sesame oil - 1/2 teaspoon
- Warm water - 1/4 cup
- Frozen peas - 3/4 cup

Preparation Time: 1 hour 15 mins

Serving Size: 6

Instructions:

1. Make the dough by mixing the flour, salt, and boiling water. Knead till you form a smooth ball and cover with a damp cloth for 1-2 hours.

2. Cook the sticky rice and set aside. In a wok, oil fry the mushrooms and shallots until they are translucent then add the scallions, wine, salt, soy sauces, five-spice powder, water, and sesame oil. Cook for a minute or two and add the rice and peas and stir it in well. Set aside to cool.

3. Cut small pieces of the dough and roll them into circles. Fill one tablespoon of filling and pleat them shut.

4. Steam for 5 minutes and serve with your favorite sauce. Enjoy!

Soup Dumplings

This two-in-one dish is so healthy and so delicious that you'll end up making it as often as you can. It has two components that meld together, the smooth, soft dumpling, and then the frozen soup that melts in the steamer inside the dumpling. Despite that, this dish is fairly simple and as long as you get the technique right, you'll be making these very frequently. Let's take a look:

Ingredients:

Aspic:

- Pork skin - ½ pound
- Pork neck bones - 1 pound
- Water - 4 cups
- Ginger - 2 slices
- Scallion - 1, cut
- Shaoxing wine - 1 tablespoon

Dough:

- All-purpose flour - 1 cup
- Warm water - 6 tablespoons

Filling:

- Ground pork - 1 pound
- Shaoxing wine - 2 tablespoons
- Salt - 3/4 teaspoon
- Sesame oil - 1/2 teaspoon
- Sugar - 3/4 teaspoon
- Light soy sauce - 3 teaspoons
- Water - 3 tablespoons
- Ground white pepper - 1/8 teaspoon
- Ginger - 1 tablespoon, minced
- Aspic - 1 ½ cup, diced

Extra:

- Chinese black vinegar - 4 tablespoons
- Fresh ginger- 2 teaspoons, julienned

Preparation Time: 1 day 30 mins

Servings size: 6

Instructions:

1. Boil the skin and bones and rinse them off to get rid of unwanted substances and then add them in a pot with the water, scallions, ginger, and wine. Bring to a boil and then simmer for two hours, covered. Then strain the liquid and allow it to cool. Once at room temperature, put it in the refrigerator overnight.

2. In a bowl, mix the dough with water slowly and knead for fifteen to twenty minutes till you get a smooth dough. Let it rest under a cloth for half an hour.

3. Make a smooth paste out of your ground pork using the food processor and then mix it with all the ingredients except the aspic. Get the mixture to be light and airy and well mixed, then fold in the aspic gently, no over-mixing. Put this in the refrigerator for easier handling.

4. Cut the dough into small pieces and roll them into small discs. Prepare the steamer.

5. Fill a tablespoon of the filling into the center of the disc and pleat it shut. Steam for eight minutes on high and serve with black vinegar and ginger. Enjoy!

I've got Fillings for You

For anyone who is looking specifically for the recipe to make the most delicious dumplings, here is the page that you have been searching for. Chinese shrimp dumplings are classic and comparatively easy to make. This dish comes together beautifully as long as you get the dough and the filling right. Here are the instructions:

Ingredients:

Dough:

- Wheat starch - 3/4 cup
- Tapioca starch - 2 tablespoons
- Salt - 1/4 teaspoon
- Boiling Water - 1/2 cup
- Vegetable oil - 2 & 1/2 teaspoons

Filling:

- Shrimp - 6 ounces
- Bamboo shoots - 3 tablespoons, finely chopped
- Green onion - 1 & 1/2 teaspoons, finely chopped
- Chinese rice wine - 3/4 teaspoon
- Sesame oil - 1/4 teaspoon
- Salt to taste
- White pepper - 1/8 teaspoon
- Egg white - 1, lightly beaten
- Cornstarch - 2 teaspoons

Preparation Time: 1 hour 15 minutes.

Serving Size: 18 dumplings

Instructions:

1. In a bowl, mix the starches and salt and add the boiling water. Knead with the oil to form a smooth dough then cover it up and rest for twenty minutes.

2. In another bowl, mix the shrimp, green onion, sesame oil, bamboo shoots, salt, rice wine, egg white, pepper and cornstarch and cover it. Rest in the refrigerator for an hour.

3. Make small circles out of the dough that is thicker at the center than the edges and spoon a tablespoon of filling into their centers. Pleat them shut and steam for fifteen minutes until translucent and the shrimps take on an orange color.

All Wrapped Up

A perfect gift for a chicken lover, this flavorsome paper-wrapped chicken is easy to make and even more fun to eat. The unwrapping process is what makes this dish an enjoyable experience, and it is a sure winner at parties. Try it out now and win some hearts!

Ingredients:

- Chicken breasts - 2 pounds
- Soy sauce - 3 tablespoons
- Oyster sauce - 3 tablespoons
- Ginger - 1 slice, shredded
- Sesame oil - 1 tablespoon
- Sherry - 1 tablespoon
- Sugar - 3 teaspoons
- Five-spice powder - 1/2 teaspoon
- Chinese dried mushrooms- 3-4, sliced into 24 pieces.
- Green onions - 3, sliced into 48 to 72 pieces.
- Cilantro - 24 sprigs
- Peanut oil - 4 cups

Preparation Time: 1 hour 45 minutes

Serving Size: 24 wraps.

Instructions:

1. Cut chicken into thin slices and pound them gently to make them tender.

2. Marinate with soy sauce, sherry, oyster sauce, five-spice powder, sugar, and some salt. Refrigerate for forty-five minutes and then add the mushrooms and green onions and let that marinate for 15 minutes.

3. Take a square parchment paper and wrap in two slices of chicken, one mushroom and two or three green onions and a sprig of cilantro.

4. Wrap it securely and then deep fry it in oil for about three minutes. The wrap is ready to serve!

Let's Make It Shiny

The next recipe that we will be trying is a special meatball recipe. Chinese Pearl Meatballs are known for their jewel-like appearance. A pearl meatball might sound hard to make, but it's easily done in just 40 minutes! This one is a great addition to the table, pleasing to both the eyes and the taste buds. Let's take a look:

Ingredients:

- Pork or beef mince - 7 ounces
- Pork fat - 4 ounces
- Dried shiitake mushrooms - 2
- Dried shrimp - 1 tablespoon
- Ginger - 2 slices, thin
- Carrot - 1, diced.
- Sticky rice - 1 ¼ cup, soaked in water for one hour
- Light soy sauce - 2 tablespoons
- Salt - ½ teaspoon
- Sugar - 2 teaspoons
- Potato starch - ½ tablespoons
- Egg - 1

Preparation Time: 40 minutes

Serving Size: 12-14

Instructions:

1. Mince the meat well and add an egg into it and mix well again. Use a food processor.

2. Soak the mushrooms and shrimp in water until soft and then chop them finely.

3. Put all the meat into a bowl and stir it unidirectionally, beating it lightly to make it springy.

4. Mix it with the mushroom, carrots, ginger, and shrimp and add the soy sauce, salt, sugar, and starch.

5. Roll into balls and cover with a layer of sticky rice.

6. Steam for fifteen minutes on high. Let them cool a little and serve warm! Enjoy!

Chinese Pork Potstickers

A potsticker is a dish that is fried in a wok and is allowed to stick lightly to the bottom to get a good glaze. This dish is insanely popular, and a slightly hardened texture at the bottom gives it a varied taste. The classic Chinese pork potsticker recipe is right here for you, take a look:

Ingredients:

Filling:

- Napa cabbage- 8 ounces
- Salt - 3 teaspoon
- Lean ground pork - 1 pound
- Green onions - 1/4 cup, finely chopped
- White wine - 1 tablespoon
- Cornstarch - 1 teaspoon
- Sesame oil - 1 teaspoon
- White pepper - 1 teaspoon

Dumplings:

- All-purpose flour - 2 cups
- Boiling water - 1 cup

Others:

- Vegetable oil - 4 tablespoons
- Water - 2 cups
- Soy sauce - 1/4 cup
- Sesame oil - 1 teaspoon

Preparation Time: 40 minutes

Serving Size: 48 dumplings

Instructions:

1. Salt the cabbage and let it rest for a while. Then squeeze out the excess moisture.

2. Mix it with the pork, wine, green onions, cornstarch, sesame oil, and pepper.

3. Knead the dough by mixing the flour and water and kneading for 5 minutes. Divide it into small balls and roll them into three-inch discs.

4. Spoon one tablespoon of filling into the center and pleat them shut.

5. Heat a wok until very hot and add some oil. Place 12 dumplings in at a time and fry for two minutes till the bottom looks golden brown.

6. Then add half a cup of water and cover and cook for six minutes.

7. Make a sauce of sesame oil and soy sauce mixed together. Serve hot. Enjoy!

A Yellow Surprise

So far, we have dealt with pork, beef, chicken, and the occasional tofu. But the star of this recipe is the ever-versatile egg, in a baked goodie that's rich, creamy, and sweet. The Hong Kong egg tart is a famous dim sum dessert served fresh out of the oven. The secret to getting this dish right is in the timing and the dough. So, let's dive right into the recipe:

Ingredients:

- All-purpose flour - 1 ½ cups
- Salt - 1/8 teaspoon
- Sugar - ½ cup + 1 tablespoon
- Unsalted butter - 14 tablespoons
- Coldwater - 2 tablespoons
- Hot water - 1 cup
- Large eggs - 3
- Evaporated milk - ½ cup
- Vanilla - 3/4 teaspoon

Preparation Time: 1 hour 40 minutes.

Serving Size: 24

Instructions:

1. Mix the dough, salt, and tablespoon of sugar. Break up the butter into the dough and mix it roughly leaving small chunks of butter in the dough. Bring it together with cold water, cover and refrigerate for twenty minutes.

2. Roll it out on your workspace away from you to make a rectangle and fold the top and bottom halves in the center, turn it left and roll it again. Cover and let it rest for thirty minutes in the refrigerator.

3. Meanwhile, dissolve the sugar in the hot water and let it come down to room temperature. Whisk together the eggs and milk, and then combine the sugar, water, and vanilla essence well. Strain it into a bowl.

4. Preheat the oven to 400 F and line the dough in your tins. Spoon in the egg mixture till it reaches the top of the crust and immediately bake it for fifteen minutes. Then lower the temperature to 350F and bake for another twelve minutes. Check if the egg mixture is baked using a toothpick; if it comes out clean, they are ready! Let it cool and enjoy!

Chinese Stuffed Tofu

Next up is a flavorsome tofu dish that is stuffed with a pork mixture. This is a very popular addition to dim sum spreads and makes a very healthy dish that is packed with intense flavors. This recipe is a Hakka style version of stuffed tofu that brings out the proteinaceous flavor of meat in all its simplicity. Here's the recipe:

Ingredients:

- Firm tofu - 1 pound
- Ground pork - 3 oz
- Salted fish - 1 oz
- Fresh ginger - 1 teaspoon
- Shaoxing wine - 2 teaspoons
- White pepper - 1/8 teaspoon
- Salt - 1/4 teaspoon
- Scallion - 1
- Oyster sauce - 1 tablespoon
- Dark soy sauce - 1 teaspoon
- Cornstarch - 1 tablespoon

Preparation Time: 30 minutes

Serving Size: 2

Instructions:

1. Mix the pork, salted fish and ginger well.

2. Cut the tofu into cubes and scoop some of it out from the center to leave a hole where the meat mixture will sit. Combine this scooped out tofu with the pork and add in some pepper, salt and wine.

3. Place the pork mix into the center of each piece and steam it for 10 minutes.

4. Pour the liquid from steaming the tofu into a saucepan and let it simmer. Then add the oyster sauce and dark soy sauce and some pepper and salt. Next, make a cornstarch slurry with cornstarch and water and add that into the sauce and let it thicken. Serve with hot steamed tofu. Enjoy!

Turnip Cake - An Interesting Twist

A cake reminds you of a sweet, decadent dessert that is every child's favorite. But if you want to go for a healthier option, we have you covered. The Chinese love this Turnip Cake made with fresh turnips or daikon radishes. What's even better about this recipe is that it's steamed! Try out this savory cake dish.

Ingredients:

- Turnip - 1
- Water - 1 ½ cups
- Oil - 2 tablespoons
- Dried shrimp - 1 tablespoon, soaked and diced.
- Dried shiitake mushrooms - 5, soaked and diced.
- Chinese sausage - 1, diced.
- Scallion - 1, chopped.
- Rice flour - 1 & 1/4 cups
- Cornstarch - 1 tablespoon
- Salt - ½ teaspoon
- Sugar - ½ teaspoon
- White pepper - ½ teaspoon
- Oyster sauce - 3-4 tablespoons

Preparation Time: 2 hours 30 minutes

Serving Size: 6

Instructions:

1. Grate the turnip and add into a wok with one and a half cups of water and let it cool down for ten minutes or more until the turnip is cooked and brown. Transfer it to a bowl with whatever water is remaining.

2. Next, stir fry the mushrooms, shrimp and Chinese sausage for five minutes and then set aside.

3. Add the cornstarch, rice flour, sugar, pepper and salt into the bowl with the turnip and water and mix well. Once well incorporated, add in the mushroom mixture and stir it in.

4. Once the batter is smooth enough, oil a pan and pour the batter into it. Steam for fifty minutes on medium-high.

5. Let it cool for half an hour and slice and serve with oyster sauce. You can also pan sear it for a few minutes to get some additional texture. Enjoy!

Clear as Crystal Dumplings

One of the most alluring things about a dumpling is its translucent appearance. You can have a good look at the filling inside and determine whether it is cooked well or not. The trick to making these near-transparent dumplings is that instead of the usually refined flour, we use potato and wheat starch that loses its opacity in the steamer. Let's take a look at this recipe.

Ingredients:

Dumplings:

- Potato starch - ½ cup + 5 teaspoons
- Wheat starch - ½ cup + 1 cup
- Water - ½ cup
- Boiling water - 1⅓ cup

Filling:

- Dried Shiitake mushrooms - 4 (soaked and diced)
- Spinach - 1½ cups
- Carrot - 1, diced
- Pork - 3 ounces, minced
- Sugar - ⅛ teaspoon
- Salt to taste
- White pepper - 1/8 teaspoon
- Sesame oil - ¼ teaspoon
- Oyster sauce - 1½ teaspoons
- Vegetable oil - 1½ teaspoons
- Cornstarch - 1 teaspoon

Preparation Time: 2 hours

Serving Size: 6

Instructions:

1. Combine the potato starch, ½ cup wheat starch and ½ cup water in a bowl. Then to the boiling water, add this mixture slowly and stir well until it solidifies.

2. Flour your workspace with 1 cup wheat starch and then knead the dough mixture until well incorporated. Let it form a smooth ball and then cover and leave it to rest.

3. Make an ice bath as well as a pot of boiling water. Blanch the spinach in the boiling water for thirty seconds or so and then transfer to an ice bath to cool. Drain them of water and then finely chop them.

4. Similarly, blanch the mushrooms and carrots for a minute and then cool them in the ice bath before draining well. Transfer to the bowl with the spinach, mix in the pork and add sugar, salt, pepper, oyster sauce, cornstarch, vegetable oil, and sesame oil. Combine well and set aside.

5. Make small three-inch circles with the dough and spoon a tablespoon of filling into the center. Pleat them shut and steam for three to four minutes on high heat. Serve with chili oil and enjoy it!

Steamed Pork Buns

Buns are traditionally baked to perfection, so you get a glossy brown outer crust and a fluffy inner part. In Chinese cooking, however, steaming is a very popular method, and they have used this technique to make the most delicious, hot and steamy buns to adorn your dim sum spread. Try out this easy, oven-free steamed pork buns recipe.

Ingredients:

Dough:

- Active dry yeast - 1 & ½ teaspoon.
- Suga r- 2 teaspoons
- Lukewarm water - 1 & 1/2 cups
- All-purpose flour - 5 cups

Filling:

- Ground pork - 1 & 1/2 pounds
- Water - 3 tablespoons
- Vegetable oil - 3 tablespoons
- Ginger - 2 tablespoons, minced
- Onion - 1, minced
- Shaoxing wine - 2 tablespoons
- Dark soy sauce - 1 tablespoon
- Sweet bean sauce - 1 tablespoon
- Ground bean sauce - 2 tablespoons
- Oyster sauce - 1 tablespoon
- Sugar - 1 teaspoon
- White pepper - 1/2 teaspoon
- Sesame oil - 2 teaspoons
- Cornstarch - 1 & 1/2 teaspoons
- Scallions - 3, chopped.

Preparation Time: 3 hours 20 minutes

Serving Size: 20

Instructions:

1. In a large bowl, mix the yeast, sugar and water and let it rest for fifteen minutes till it foams.

2. Then mix the dough half a cup at a time and knead till it forms a smooth ball. Cover and set it in a warm area to let it proof for 1 hour.

3. Mix the pork with three tablespoons of water. In a pan, heat the oil and cook onions and ginger until onions become translucent. Next add in the pork and cook it till the meat turns pale.

4. Next add all the seasonings from wine to the sesame oil one by one and cook it down until no water remains. Make a cornstarch slurry with one tablespoon water and pour that into the mixture. Let it thicken and then set aside to cool. Fold in the scallions.

5. Knead the dough for two minutes to rid any air bubbles and divide it into twenty equal pieces. Make circles out of each piece that is thicker at the center and thin at the edges and pipe in some filling at the center. Pleat it shut and place it on your steaming tray and let it proof for another fifteen minutes.

6. Once proofed, start with cold water in your steamer and set it on medium-high heat. Steam for fifteen minutes and then turn off the heat. Keep the lid on for an extra five to seven minutes before taking it out of the basket or they will fall apart. Serve warm and enjoy!

Zhaliang - Bread Rolls Reinvented

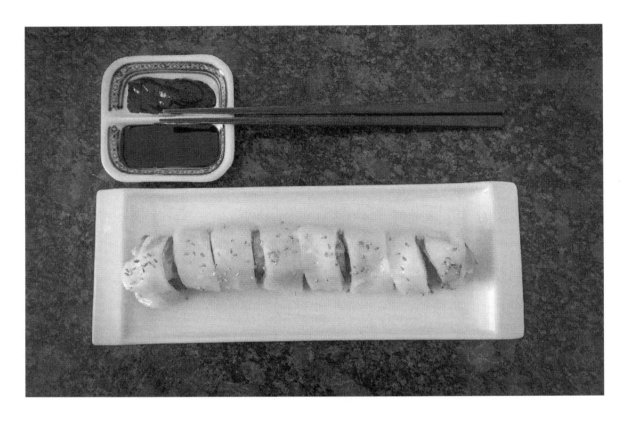

Who doesn't love a nice juicy bread roll? In Chinese cooking, equivalent to the traditional bread roll is the Zhaliang, a rice noodle roll covering the Chinese breadstick or Youtiao. You can easily get Youtiao at the local Asian market and spice it up a notch with this delicious Zhaliang and the recipe is easy to make.

Ingredients:

Sauce:

- Scallion - 1, white part
- Ginger - 1 piece
- Light soy sauce - 2 1/2 tablespoons
- Dark soy sauce - 2 teaspoons
- Sugar - 5 teaspoons
- Water - 1/3 cup
- Oyster sauce - 1 teaspoon
- Oil - 1 teaspoon
- Salt - to taste

Zhejiang:

- Youtiao - 1
- Rice flour - 5 tablespoons
- Mung bean starch - 1 tablespoon
- Wheat starch - 2 tablespoons
- Cornstarch - 2 tablespoons
- Salt - 1/4 teaspoon
- Water - 1 cup
- Vegetable oil - 2 tablespoons

Preparation Time: 1 hour

Serving Size: 6

Instructions:

1. Make the sauce by adding all ingredients to a pan and letting it simmer over low heat. Once cooled, remove the chunks of solid materials and let it rest.

2. Cut the youtiao in half and reheat the pieces in a toaster oven or preheated regular oven until it becomes a tad crispy, for five to six minutes.

3. Mix the rice flour, wheat starch, salt and mung bean starch in a bowl. Add water and mix till no lumps remain and let it rest to get rid of any air bubbles.

4. Soak a cotton cloth in water and also prepare your countertop by oiling it well for assembly of the roll. To steam rice noodles, use a sheet pan.

5. Line the cotton cloth on the pan and pour the noodle batter into it such that the cloth is just enveloped. Lower it into the steamer and take care to keep it leveled for uniform thickness of the rice noodle. Steam on high for two minutes and take it out.

6. Turn the pan upside down on your oiled surface such that the noodles touch the counter. Separate the noodles from the cloth using a scraper while both are still hot, do not worry about any aberrations.

7. Line one youtiao piece at the edge of the noodle and roll it up. Slice into pieces and serve with the sauce. Enjoy!

Bamboozled

As we near the end of this cookbook, we have decided to include one such recipe that takes the essence of Chinese cooking and incorporates it into a seemingly easy dish. The Cantonese Style rice dumplings are different, flavorsome, and take more than a day of preparation. You will be using bamboo leaves that impart a classic Asian flavor to the dish. Take a look.

Ingredients:

- Dried bamboo leaves - 40
- Uncooked sticky rice - 5 cups
- Light soy sauce - 2 tablespoons + 2 teaspoons
- Salt - to taste
- Raw peanuts - 2/3 cup
- Pork belly - 1 pound, 12 pieces.
- Sugar - 1/2 teaspoon
- Shaoxing wine - 2 teaspoons
- White pepper - 1/2 teaspoon
- Oil - 1 teaspoon
- Water - ½ cup
- Salted duck egg yolks - 6
- Chinese sausages - 3

Preparation Time: 1 day 8 hours

Serving Size: 12

Instructions:

1. Soak the leaves overnight and then wash them on both sides the next day. Keep them in water till the time you use them.

2. Soak the sticky rice overnight and the next day, drain it, mix with two teaspoons of soy sauce and salt.

3. Soak the raw peanuts overnight and next day boil for five minutes, then drain them and keep it aside.

4. Mix the pork with wine, salt, sugar, soy sauce, and pepper and refrigerate overnight.

5. Next day, cook the pork belly in oil for a few minutes, then add the water and cover and let it cook until all the water is gone. Set aside.

6. Cut the eggs and sausage into 12 pieces.

7. To wrap the, cut off half an inch of the leaves from the bottom. Line two or three leaves together and fold the bottom to form a cone.

8. Layer some rice, and the pork belly, peanuts, sausage, and eggs. Add some more rice to cover it and fold in the leaves to make a secure packet. Tie it up with twine.

9. Put these into a pot and place a heavy plate on it. Cover with water and let it simmer for seven to eight hours. If it dries up, add more boiling water.

10. Serve them hot and enjoy it!

Go Green

To end this beautiful journey that was filled with various Chinese dishes and techniques, we have chosen an easy, classic Chinese ingredient. Stuffed capsicum or green bell pepper is an extremely healthy addition to your menu. Even better, it's super easy to make. Here's a thirty-minute thirtieth recipe.

Ingredients:

- Shrimp - 12 ounces
- Scallions - 2
- Salt - 1 teaspoon
- Vegetable oil - 2 tablespoons
- Sesame oil - 1/2 teaspoon
- Cornstarch - 1 ½ tablespoons
- Shaoxing wine - 2 teaspoons
- White pepper - 1 teaspoon
- Bell peppers - 3
- Oil - 1 tablespoon

Sauce:

- Oil - 1 tablespoon
- Garlic - 1 clove, minced
- Fermented Black Beans - 1 tablespoon
- Shaoxing wine - 1 teaspoon
- Chicken stock - 1 cup
- Salt - ¼ teaspoon
- Sugar - ¼ teaspoon
- Soy sauce - 1 teaspoon
- Oyster sauce - 1 teaspoon
- Cornstarch - 1 tablespoon

Preparation Time: 30 minutes

Serving Size: 4

Instructions:

1. Chop the Shrimp into a very nice paste.

2. Add some of the chopped scallions to the shrimp, mix in wine, salt, pepper, vegetable and sesame oil along with cornstarch. Whip this mixture until well combined.

3. Cut the bell peppers into three or five segments and remove seeds. Fill it with a shrimp mixture.

4. Oil fry the bell peppers in oil, on both sides until tender and well cooked.

5. To make the sauce, cook the fermented black beans in oil and garlic for a few seconds, then add the wine. Once the wine is reduced and bubbles are formed, add-in chicken stock, salt, sugar, oyster sauce, and soy sauce. Let it simmer and then make a cornstarch slurry and add that into the sauce. Let it thicken up and then serve on top of the peppers. Enjoy!

Conclusion

Chinese cooking is an art that requires mastery over a lot of techniques, including dough making, working the steamer, and even in the way you stir a mixture. To perfect this art, the best way is to practice until you are fluent. In this cookbook, we have seen multiple new techniques and methods and used a lot of new ingredients and flavors. Some recipes took over a day, and some took just twenty minutes. But overall, at the end of this cookbook, you would have dabbled in the culinary techniques of the Chinese and made a few delicious dim sum recipes that will make you a beloved cook among family and friends.

We hope you found this journey an exciting challenge!

About the Author

Ivy's mission is to share her recipes with the world. Even though she is not a professional cook she has always had that flair toward cooking. Her hands create magic. She can make even the simplest recipe tastes superb. Everyone who has tried her food has astounding their compliments was what made her think about writing recipes.

She wanted everyone to have a taste of her creations aside from close family and friends. So, deciding to write recipes was her winning decision. She isn't interested in popularity, but how many people have her recipes reached and touched people. Each recipe in her cookbooks is special and has a special meaning in her life. This means that each recipe is created with attention and love. Every ingredient carefully picked, every combination tried and tested.

Her mission started on her birthday about 9 years ago, when her guests couldn't stop prizing the food on the table. The next thing she did was organizing an event where chefs from restaurants were tasting her recipes. This event gave her the courage to start spreading her recipes.

She has written many cookbooks and she is still working on more. There is no end in the art of cooking; all you need is inspiration, love, and dedication.

Author's Afterthoughts

I am thankful for downloading this book and taking the time to read it. I know that you have learned a lot and you had a great time reading it. Writing books is the best way to share the skills I have with your and the best tips too.

I know that there are many books and choosing my book is amazing. I am thankful that you stopped and took time to decide. You made a great decision and I am sure that you enjoyed it.

I will be even happier if you provide honest feedback about my book. Feedbacks helped by growing and they still do. They help me to choose better content and new ideas. So, maybe your feedback can trigger an idea for my next book.

Thank you again

Sincerely

Ivy Hope

Printed in Great Britain
by Amazon